Christmas Carols for Cello

Christmas Carols for Cello
Easy Songs in First Position!

Christmas Carols for Cello: Easy Songs in First Position!
© 2012 by Javier Marcó

ISBN-13:978-1481004268
ISBN-10:1481004263

This Christmas I've got a lot of gifts for you!

and also...

We're going to play and sing christmas carols together!

Contents

Playing Guide 15

A la Nanita Nana 21

Adestes Fidelis 22

Away in a Manger 23

Ça, Bergers, assemblons nous 24

Campana sobre Campana 25

Campanita de Lugar 26

Fröhliche Weihnacht überall 28

Hark! The Herald Sing 29

Il est né, le divin Enfant! 30

Jingle Bells 31

Joy To The World 33

La marche des Rois 34

Leise rieselt der Schnee 35

Les Anges dans nos Campagnes 36

Los Peces en el Río 37

Minuit, chrétiens 38

O Tannenbaum 40

Still, Still, Still 41

Stille Nacht, heilige Nacht 42

The First Nowel 43

Tu scendi dalle stele 44

We Wish You A Merry Christmas 45

Playing guide

Standard notation
Notes are written on a Staff.

Staff
The staff consists of five lines and four spaces, on which notes symbols are placed.

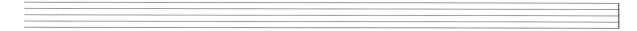

Clef
A clef assigns an individual note to a certain line. The **Bass Clef** or **F Clef** is used for the cello.

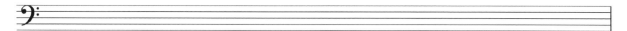

This clef indicates the position of the note F which is on the line between the two dots.

Note
A note is a sign used to represent the relative pitch of a sound. There are seven notes: A, B, C, D, E, F and G.

Ledger lines
The ledger lines are used to inscribe notes outside the lines and spaces of the staff.

Accidentals
An accidental is a symbol to raise or lower the pitch of a note.

♯ sharp   Next note down half step.

♭ flat   Next note up half step.

♮ natural   Cancels a flat or a sharp.

15

Note values

A **note value** is used to indicate the duration of a note. A **rest** is an interval of silence, marked by a sign indicating the length of the pause. Each rest corresponds to a particular note value.

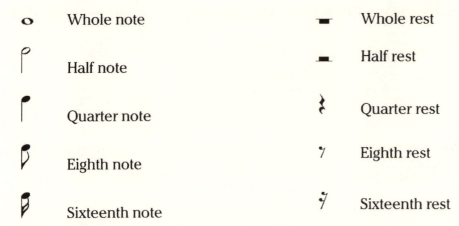

Dotted note

A dotted note is a note with a small dot written after it. The dot adds half as much again to the basic note's duration.

Tie

A tie is a curved line connecting the heads of two notes of the same pitch, indicating that they are to be played as a single note with a duration equal to the sum of the individual notes' note values.

Bars or Measures

The staff is divided into equal segments of time consisting of the same number of beats, called bar or measures.

Time signature

Time signature consists of two numbers, the upper number specifies how many beats (or counts) are in each measure, and the lower number tells us the note value which represents one beat.

Example: 4/4 means four quarters, or four beats per measure with a quarter note receiving one beat or count.

Key signature
A Key signature is a group of accidentals, generally written at the beginning of a score immediately after the clef, and shows which notes always get sharps or flats. Accidentals on the lines and spaces in the key signature affect those notes throughout the piece unless there is a natural sign.

Repeat sign
The repeat sign indicates a section should be repeated from the beginning, and then continue on. A corresponding sign facing the other way indicates where the repeat is to begin.

First and second endings
The section should be repeated from the beginning, and number brackets above the bars indicate which to played the first time (1), which to play the second time (2).

Fingering
In this book left hand fingering is indicated using numbers above the staff.
0= open
1= index
2= middle
3= ring
4= little finger

Bowings

Down-bow   Up-bow

Slur
Indicates that two or more notes are to be played in one bow.

17

Dynamics

Dynamics refers to the volume of the notes.

p (piano), meaning soft.
mp (mezzo-piano), meaning "moderately soft".
mf (mezzo-forte), meaning "moderately loud".
f (forte), meaning loud.

⎯⎯⎯⎯⎯⎯ Crescendo. A gradual increase in volume.

⎯⎯⎯⎯⎯⎯ Decrescendo. A gradual decrease in volume.

Tempo Markings

Tempo is written at the beginning of a piece of music and indicates how slow or fast this piece should be played.

Lento — very slow (40–60 bpm)
Adagio — slow and stately (66–76 bpm)
Andate — at a walking pace (76–108 bpm)
Moderato — moderately (101-110 bpm)
Allegro — fast, quickly and bright (120–139 bpm)
Allegretto — moderately fast (but less so than allegro)
Alla marcia — in the manner of a march
In tempo di valse — in tempo of vals

rallentando — gradual slowing down
a tempo — returns to the base tempo after a *rallentando*

Articulation

Legato. Notes are played smoothly and connected.

Stacatto. Notes are played separated or detached from its neighbours by a silence.

Fermata (pause)

The note is to be prolonged at the pleasure of the performer.

A la Nanita Nana

Tradicional
Arr: Javier Marcó

Adeste Fideles

John Francis Wade
Arr: Javier Marcó

Away in a Manger

James Ramsey Murray
Arr: Javier Marcó

Ça, Bergers, assemblons nous

James Ramsey Murray
Arr: Javier Marcó

Campana sobre Campana

Tradicional
Arr: Javier Marcó

Campanita del Lugar

Tradicional
Arr: Javier Marcó

Fröhliche Weihnacht überall

Traditionell
Arr: Javier Marcó

Hark! The Herald Angels Sing

Felix Mendelssohn
Arr. Javier Marcó

Allegro

Il est né, le divin Enfant!

Traditionnel
Arr: Javier Marcó

Jingle Bells

James Lord Pierpont
Arr. Javier Marcó

Joy To The World

Georg Friedrich Händel
Arr. Javier Marcó

La marche des Rois

Georges Bizet
Arr: Javier Marcó

Allegro

Leise rieselt der Schnee

Eduard Ebel
Arr. Javier Marcó

35

Les Anges dans nos Campagnes

Traditionnel
Arr: Javier Marcó

Los Peces en el Río

Tradicional
Arr: Javier Marcó

Moderato

Minuit, chrétiens

Adolphe Adam
Arr: Javier Marcó

O Tannenbaum

Traditionell
Arr: Javier Marcó

Still, Still, Still

Traditionell
Arr: Javier Marcó

Andante

Stille Nacht, heilige Nacht

Franz Xaver Gruber
Arr. Javier Marcó

The First Nowell

Traditional
Arr. Javier Marcó

Tu scendi dalle stelle

Alfonso María de Ligorio
Arr: Javier Marcó

Allegro

We Wish You A Merry Christmas

Traditional
Arr. Javier Marcó

Presto

Please visit our website to find more titles of our catalog:
www.MarcoMusica.com

Merry Christmas and a happy New Year!

Made in the USA
Middletown, DE
03 December 2018